The Truth About You

*The Easy Guide to Share Your Life Story
through Video, Audio, or the Written Word*

Brian Vaszily

To my dad, William Victor Vaszily, who died decades ago and whose life I now dearly wish I knew much more about.

Table of Contents

The Truth About You

A Life Story – The Ultimate Gift

Think about your mother, your father, grandparents, great-grandparents, and other special and significant people in your family and life for a moment. Whether they're here with you or gone from this world, whose life would you love to know more about?

How much would you cherish being handed a book written in their own hand? Perhaps an audio featuring their voice? Even a video of them speaking directly to you, where they reveal the most fascinating and worthwhile details of their lives, such as:

- Their first-hand description of the house they grew up in as a child
- The greatest dreams and fears they had
- What their parents, grandparents, and siblings were like
- The friends they played with, what they played with, how they played
- The romantic details of how they met their significant other
- Their personal recollections of wartime and other historic events
- The clothes they wore, the entertainment they enjoyed, the work they did
- Their health challenges and how they faced them
- Their personal advice on how to best live life
- And so much more!

The more mature you are, the more likely you agree that nothing matters more than family and loved ones. The typical gifts we give one another to show our love may be good, but *nothing* could hold more meaning or be more cherished than the <u>story of someone's own life</u>.

It is truly the ultimate gift.

We can't turn back the clock to receive this gift – these first-hand accounts – from the dearly departed, of course. (It's possible to capture some stories of the dearly departed from those still living who knew them…but it isn't the same, is it?) So please consider this:

Right now, and certainly in the future, your loved ones will greatly appreciate hearing the truth about you. **Your life story.**

Now some people may get humble here and think, "Who would want to know more about *me*?" That's probably what your ancestors thought, and yet how you'd love to know their stories today!

The fact is, your children, grandchildren, great-grandchildren, great-great-grandchildren, nieces, nephews, and others in your bloodline will cherish your gift – your legacy, your life story – likely more than anything else you can leave them!

Start a Trend

Can you think of living family members and friends who ought to be recording *their* life stories? So they can share them with current family and future generations?

Often when thinking about that question, family and friends who have done or lived through something particularly amazing first come to mind.

But the truth is, everyone has a story to tell. Their greatest hardships and greatest joys. Their romances and heartbreaks. Their beliefs and how they viewed the world. All the *stuff* of the world that surrounded them, from big news events to items they collected, from the books they read to the food they ate.

Your story is who you are.

This book is the ideal gift for two very important reasons.

First, you can gift it to others who *really* ought to record their histories for posterity.

Second, it's a book whose result – the *key pieces* of who you are – will be cherished as an heirloom by family now and for generations to come.

Even if you live to be one hundred and nine (and I hope you do!), your life up to now is your story. <u>Don't wait to tell it</u>. You don't want to postpone recording and sharing it "someday," because tomorrow isn't guaranteed to anyone.

Your personal story is amazing, important, and worth sharing. You'll only realize this more as you answer the questions in this book.

There's also an additional benefit to answering the questions and it may surprise you.

Whether you're answering on your own or embarking on the journey with a loved one, recalling the facts, memories, thoughts, wishes, and beliefs of your life centers you, broadens your self-awareness, and fills you with feelings of peace and happiness.

Taking a walk through the history of yourself reminds you about things that are important and may help you find closure with your past. It may even inspire you to reconnect with people who've fallen out of touch. That's all a wonderful *bonus gift* indeed!

The Simple Instructions

Whether you will be answering these questions on your own or guiding a loved one through them, you will first need to decide how you will record the answers. There are three basic options:

- Writing
- Audio
- Video

Writing tends to take longer, but can result in more interesting answers, as the concentrated act of writing has been proven to aid in recalling memories and details. Audio and video may not have the same effect.

Writing your answers out is also a form of journaling, which has been shown to reduce stress and boost feelings of calm and happiness. Some people may enjoy this book for the therapeutic benefits alone!

The questions in this book have white space after them so you can write your answers here if you choose. (You can also use the space for making notes about the questions that you can refer to later, including if you choose to video or audio record.)

Alternately you can choose to write or type out your answers on other paper. If you intend to make multiple copies of your life story to hand out to family and friends, you may want to use a paper medium that is easy to photocopy, such as the pages of this book or a spiral bound notebook.

Also remember that some people may have handwriting that's challenging for others to read. And many people from younger generations are no longer taught how to read cursive writing at all. These are a few considerations for typing answers on the computer instead, having handwritten answers transcribed to the computer, or choosing audio or video recording.

Audio is the obvious choice for those who may not have the time or energy to write out their answers and who don't want to appear on camera.

Speaking into an audio recording device is also good for focusing people more deeply inward, inside their hearts and minds, when answering the questions. There's no camera to distract them or make them feel self-conscious. Plus, it's more mobile, as there is no need to stare at a screen when recording.

Video offers obvious benefits to those who will view it in the future. You're able to be seen and heard. Viewers can see the subject in action as they share stories from their life.

You learn a lot by watching facial expression, body language, and listening to tone and style of speaking. This may be as priceless to future generations as the stories themselves. If one isn't comfortable being filmed, though, this option might make the subject feel nervous or stilted in their answers. If you truly want to go the video route anyway, keep trying and give ample time to get comfortable and "forget" the camera.

Current Technology Is Your Friend

From a technology perspective, any of these mediums are easy to accomplish today.

Choosing to journal your answers can be done with pen here in the book or on separate paper, or by typing into a simple word processing program.

Both audio and video can be easily accomplished with a smart phone, tablet, or computer and produced with excellent quality. These files are easy to upload from your device to free websites such as YouTube. You can store them privately and opt to share them with friends and family as you choose.

There are also many *free* or *very-low-cost* applications available online that you can download to your phone or computer to record longer sessions. Search for terms such as <u>long-form audio recording app for Android</u> or long-form audio recording app <u>for iPhone</u> to find the latest and greatest of those.

Tasty Bite-Size Pieces

Whether you choose to record your own or a loved one's life story in writing, audio, video, or a combination of all three, <u>here's the most important thing to remember about the entire process</u>:

Don't stress yourself out about it. Keep it enjoyable!

Don't try to complete recording an entire life story in a single day, or even a few days. Your life didn't happen in a day or a week, so recording it in such a span can prove to be difficult.

Take it in bite-size pieces. It's more digestible and delicious that way!

By breaking this up into smaller sections, it will give you time to truly explore what you want to say. This will result in deeper and more interesting answers. Commit to answering a handful of questions at a time versus trying to race through and answer as many questions as possible.

You can choose to do this two ways:

- Review all the sections and questions in this book before you start to answer them. Prioritize what you feel is most important to answer in the order you want it answered.

  For example, everyone enjoys a good love story. Perhaps you'll want to spend the first session answering the Youthful Love questions and the Romantic Relationships questions before moving on to other questions in other sessions. If you're recording answers from the very elderly or sick, their energy levels may only allow for small sessions and prioritizing is key.

- Move through answering the questions you want to answer chronologically. You can take one sub-section per session and complete it before moving on.

If you choose to record your life story in video or audio, you'll likely have multiple video or audio files from each session you recorded.

These files tend to take a lot of memory, so consider uploading them to a site like YouTube. It frees up memory on your device and gives you a safe backup option.

As you upload them, choose a method of titling your files to keep them organized and to make it easy for you and others to find those you are seeking (for example: **Brian Vaszily - Session 4 - Jobs and Careers**).

When your story is complete, you might opt to have the multiple files put together in one large presentation such as a PowerPoint slide show or a DVD.

If you do this yourself or have it done professionally, though, be sure to break it up into easily identifiable sections or chapters – such as **Youth, Marriage**, etc. – to make it easy for others to jump to the sections they want to see or hear.

A few more suggestions on this front:

- Movie editing applications such as iMovie (or audio editing applications such as GarageBand), make it fairly easy to create quality presentations yourself. While easy is a relative term, if you're comfortable working with basic technology or software, you should find them user-friendly.

- Hire someone to edit your video or audio for you. Search for audio/video editing on websites such as Fiverr.com who bring together pros worldwide willing to perform services like this (and many more) at prices fit for the tightest of budgets.

  For a little extra money, many service providers are happy to go a long way in customizing your video or audio, too. For example, you could add digital photos to an audio file so listeners can enjoy the photos as a life story is being shared.

They can even incorporate background music of your favorite songs, and much more. The ideas are limitless.

With all of the above in mind, don't let planning and concerns about the end result get in the way of recording your (or a loved one's) life story. Making sure you tell the **Truth About You** is the most important thing. Fancy it up to your heart's desire later!

A Love Letter

One more important reminder before you jump in.

This is not a test and you won't be graded. There are no right or wrong answers to the following questions. You're under no obligation to try to impress anyone, nor are you expected to be falsely modest.

Give yourself permission to tell the **Truth About You** as you see fit.

Pondering and answering the following questions can be quite enjoyable and calming, so the key is to let that enjoyment shine through…and babble if you want to!

I have a few tips for you to keep in mind as you go along. They're listed in the next section. They'll simplify the process and make it easier for you to keep going.

But the only real *rule* is to relax and be yourself.

With all of the joys and challenges you've faced, with all the feelings you've felt, and the lessons you've learned…your life has *already* been an amazing journey that's worth sharing.

Your recorded answers to any and all of these questions are ultimately a love letter to your family now and in the future. What they'll most appreciate and benefit from is simply getting the **Truth About You**.

Enjoy the experience of creating this unique gift for them.

Sharing Your Story – 10 Important Tips

When you're ready to begin, use these **10 Life Story Tips** to make the process, and the end result, more enjoyable.

LIFE STORY TIP #1:

If you're guiding someone through these questions, gently nurture more information from them by asking additional questions based on an answer they give.

For example, let's say you asked, "If you could tell your mother anything or ask her anything and get an answer today from her, what would you say or ask her?"

And they answered, "I would tell her how much I love her."

You may then want to ask, "Are those words you said to one another a lot when she was alive?"

This is a common practice journalists employ to get to the more interesting details.

LIFE STORY TIP #2:

Consider adding pictures from various points of your life to your written or video recording.

For example, you could include pictures of you and your brothers and sisters, from when you were young to now, with your answers in the **Your Siblings** section.

LIFE STORY TIP #3:

When answering these questions, don't worry about saying the *right* thing and don't worry about perfection (there's no such thing). If you find yourself freezing up on questions, it's likely because you're thinking too hard about them.

Instead consider this an easygoing conversation and let whatever wants to flow out of your mouth or fingertips flow out! If additional information pops into your head later for a given question, there are no laws against going back to add it later.

LIFE STORY TIP #4:

Don't hold back! If you want to reveal a story or insight from your life but the question that would lead to it is not included in this book, go right ahead and reveal that story or insight.

While 400 of the biggest questions to peel away the layers of anyone's life story are included here, everyone's life is unique. There will likely be unique aspects of your life worth revealing that aren't specifically asked about here. Add them!

LIFE STORY TIP #5:

Several of the questions throughout this book ask what your favorite songs were at various phases of your life.

Consider adding these songs, or snippets of them, to your audio or video recording. Have a CD made of those favorite songs to be saved and included with your written answers.

LIFE STORY TIP #6:

Are you guiding someone through these questions and doing an audio recording of it? If you take frequent car rides with them, that's a wonderful opportunity to have them answer questions with a digital audio recorder present. Make sure you always keep your hands on the wheel and eyes on the road, please!

LIFE STORY TIP #7:

Remember, you don't have to try to answer *every single question* in this guide. Instead, read through the questions in a given section and answer those that most call out to you.

If you're pressed for time, choose 25 from the entire guide you want to answer most. You can do another 25 when you have more time later.

LIFE STORY TIP #8:

Whether you're guiding someone through the book or answering them yourself, the end result is going to be fascinating. Make copies of the written, audio, or video finished product to give to loved ones. They'll be one of the most cherished gifts they ever receive and it will be something passed forward through the generations.

This may include making a cover that includes standout quotes from the answers to the questions, photos, or even drawings from your children or grandchildren.

LIFE STORY TIP #9:

Know anyone who loves scrapbooking? If you're writing your answers to the questions, consider giving them to such a person along with photos and perhaps other paper mementos from your life. This might include copies of your birth and marriage certificates, the invitation to your wedding, your school report cards, etc.

They can then turn it all into a beautiful work of biographical art! If you don't know anyone who enjoys this hobby, there are many scrapbooking services you can search out online. However, make sure you use a reputable source or choose what documents you share carefully.

LIFE STORY TIP #10:

In the **Military** and **Jobs and Careers** sections, there are a lot of other stories and insights worth revealing that are not asked here because they may be particular to your line of work and experience. Consider adding them to the **Additional Notes** in the back of the book.

For example, if you were a cook in the military, you likely have a range of interesting stories and insights about the type of food you typically cooked and the biggest kitchen disaster you ever had. If you were or are a physician, you probably have many stories such as the strangest injuries you've ever seen and more.

Your family and future generations would love to hear these, so as always opt for telling as much as you can versus holding anything back!

LIFE STORY BONUS TIP:

Relax, be yourself, and have fun with it. This isn't a test and it shouldn't be a chore. Your life story or that of a loved one should fill you with happiness. Embrace it and get started!

Section One: Your Formative Years

Let's start with some foundational information about you. This section focuses on your immediate family and things you remember from childhood.

Be as specific as possible and use the extra space at the end of each chapter for additional thoughts or notes. You can also use the space at the end of the book.

Basics About You

What's your full name? If relevant, what's your maiden name and/or other last names?

_____

_____

_____

_____

Do you know why you were given your first and middle names? What (if anything) is the significance of these names?

_____

_____

_____

_____

Did you or do you have any nicknames or pet names that others often called you? What were they, who used them, and why?

_____

_____

_____

_____

What month, day, and year were you born?

_____

_____

_____

What city, state, or Provence were you born in? What hospital were you born in, or were you born at home?

_____

_____

_____

What's your racial and ethnic background?

_____

_____

_____

_____

What's your religion and denomination, if any? Did you ever switch religions and denominations? Why?

_____

_____

_____

_____

_____

Additional Notes

Additional Notes

Family Ties

Parents are among the most influential people in anyone's life. The questions in the following sections are about mothers and fathers, but if someone else played a significant role in raising you, please note that relationship and also answer the same questions for them.

For example, if you had adoptive parents or you were raised in large part by stepparents or foster parents, please note that and answer the questions for all of them.

Where, when and how did your parents first meet one another?

_____

_____

_____

If your parents got married, what date did they get married. How long did they stay married?

_____

_____

_____

Do you know where they were married and where they honeymooned?

_____

_____

_____

If your parents got divorced or one was widowed, when was that and how old were you?

_____

_____

_____

Please describe the circumstances and how it impacted you.

_____

_____

_____

_____

_____

What was your parents' relationship with one another like?

_____

_____

_____

_____

_____

_____

_____

If your parents remarried, what were your stepparents like? What were their names? What kind of relationship did you have with them?

_____

_____

_____

_____

_____

_____

_____

_____

Did any of your parents serve in the military, fight in any wars, or were they directly involved in any historic events?

_____

_____

_____

_____

_____

_____

_____

_____

Additional Notes

Your Mother

What's your mother's name, maiden name, place of birth, and birthday? If she has passed away, when was that?

_____

_____

_____

How would you describe your mother's appearance?

_____

_____

_____

In terms of her character, how would you describe your mother?

_____

_____

_____

_____

_____

_____

_____

What kind of work did your mother primarily do?

What were some of her favorite hobbies and pastimes?

What types of clothes did your mother wear around the house, at work, or for special occasions?

What were some of your mother's favorite musicians, songs, TV shows, and movies?

_____

_____

_____

_____

_____

_____

What do you remember most fondly about your mother when you were young?

_____

_____

_____

_____

_____

_____

What did you find most difficult or challenging about your mother?

_____

_____

_____

_____

_____

_____

In what ways would you say you're most like your mother? In what ways would you say you're most different?

_____

_____

_____

_____

_____

_____

_____

_____

_____

Describe your fondest outing or situation with your mother.

_____

_____

_____

_____

_____

_____

What are the most important things you learned from your mother?

_____

_____

_____

_____

_____

_____

_____

_____

_____

_____

_____

_____

If your mother passed away, do you recall what she died of?

_____

_____

_____

_____

If you could tell your mother anything or ask her anything and get an answer today from her, what would you say or ask her? Why?

_____

_____

_____

_____

_____

_____

_____

_____

_____

_____

_____

_____

_____

_____

_____

_____

"An ounce of mother is worth a pound of clergy."

Rudyard Kipling

Additional Notes

Additional Notes

Your Father

What was your father's name, place of birth, and birthday? If he has passed away, when was that?

_____

_____

_____

In terms of his physical appearance, how would you describe your father?

_____

_____

_____

In terms of his character, how would you describe your father?

_____

_____

_____

_____

_____

_____

What kind of work did your father do?

_____

_____

_____

_____

What were some of his favorite hobbies and pastimes?

_____

_____

_____

_____

_____

_____

_____

_____

What types of clothes did your father wear around the house, to work, or for special occasions?

_____

_____

_____

_____

_____

_____

What were some of your father's favorite musicians, songs, TV shows, and movies?

What do you remember most fondly about your father?

What did you find most difficult or challenging about your father when you were younger?

_____

_____

_____

_____

_____

_____

In what ways would you say you're most like your father? In what ways would you say you're most different?

_____

_____

_____

_____

_____

_____

_____

_____

_____

_____

_____

Describe your fondest outing or situation with your father.

_____

_____

_____

_____

_____

_____

What are the most important things you learned from your father?

_____

_____

_____

_____

_____

_____

If your father passed away, do you recall what he died of?

_____

_____

_____

If you could tell your father anything or ask him anything and get an answer from him today, what would you say or ask? Why?

_____

_____

_____

_____

_____

_____

_____

_____

_____

_____

_____

_____

_____

_____

_____

_____

"My daddy, he was somewhere between God and John Wayne."

Hank Williams, Jr.

Additional Notes

Additional Notes

Your Siblings

If you have them, brothers and sisters can play a remarkably important role in your life. For the following questions, also answer for any half-siblings, step-siblings, or foster siblings you may have. Please note the relationship.

What are the names of your siblings, their birthdays, and are they older or younger?

_____

_____

_____

_____

_____

Describe the character of your siblings.

_____

_____

_____

_____

_____

_____

_____

_____

Were you close to some or all of your siblings? Which ones, why, and why not the others?

What did you love or appreciate the most about your siblings?

What did you dislike about your siblings?

It is almost a given that siblings will fight and argue. What did you and your siblings fight and argue about most?

What did you envy about your siblings, from physical traits to personality?

Describe a situation or two where you were especially grateful to any of your siblings, such as situations where they went above and beyond to help you out of a bind?

Describe your favorite games and ways of playing with your siblings when you were little.

What type of work did your siblings do in their life?

_____

_____

_____

_____

_____

_____

_____

Did your siblings get married and have families? Note their spouses' and children's names.

_____

_____

_____

_____

_____

_____

_____

_____

_____

If they've passed away, do you recall when and what your siblings died of?

_____

_____

_____

_____

_____

What were your thoughts and feelings regarding their passing?

_____

_____

_____

_____

_____

What conflicts do you wish you could or would have resolved with your siblings?

_____

_____

_____

_____

_____

_____

Is there anything you wish you could say or could have said to any of them?

_____

_____

_____

_____

_____

_____

_____

_____

_____

_____

_____

_____

_____

_____

_____

_____

_____

_____

"Your parents leave you too soon and your kids and spouse
come along late, but your siblings know you
when you are in your most inchoate form."

Jeffrey Kluger

Additional Notes

Your Grandparents

Some grandparents play a central and warm role in people's youths, while others may be more distant. Either way, they're typically our most prominent link to events that seem like ancient history and to viewpoints that seem either outdated or very wise, depending on who's listening.

What were the names of your grandparents (and great-grandparents if possible)? If you can recall, where were they born and what were their birthdays?

_____

_____

_____

_____

_____

Did you personally know your grandparents? Your great-grandparents? Were you close?

_____

_____

_____

_____

_____

How would you describe the character of the grandparents and great-grandparents you knew?

_____

_____

_____

_____

_____

_____

_____

_____

Do you know how your grandmother first met your grandfather on each side of your family? Do you know when they were married and how long their marriage lasted?

_____

_____

_____

_____

_____

_____

_____

_____

Do you recall what your grandparents and great-grandparents primarily did as careers?

_____

_____

_____

_____

_____

What do you recall about your grandparents' homes? For example, what was the furniture and décor like, what did the home smell like, what was in the backyard, and other details?

_____

_____

_____

_____

_____

Did your grandparents have habits or character traits that seemed unusual, amusing, or intimidating to you?

_____

_____

_____

_____

_____

What type of music, TV shows, movies, books, newspapers, and magazines do you recall your grandparents enjoying?

_____

_____

_____

_____

_____

_____

_____

Did any of them serve in the military and were they involved in any wars? If so, do you recall stories from the military and war that they may have shared with you?

_____

_____

_____

_____

_____

_____

_____

_____

Were your grandparents involved in any historical events to your recollection?

_____

_____

_____

_____

_____

_____

_____

_____

What fascinating or interesting stories do you recall your grandparents about your blood relations from long ago, such as their parents, grandparents, or beyond?

_____

_____

_____

_____

_____

_____

_____

_____

_____

_____

Did they share stories of long-ago family involved in scandals or who were members of royalty?

_____

_____

_____

_____

_____

_____

_____

_____

_____

For any of them who've passed away, do you recall when and what each died from?

_____

_____

_____

_____

_____

_____

_____

_____

_____

Did they give you advice or do anything you're particularly grateful for and what was it?

Additional Notes

Your Extended Family & Family Friends

Whether you had frequent interactions or not, relationships and experiences with aunts, uncles, cousins, and other family members beyond the nuclear family can be some of the most influential and memorable aspects of youth.

How many aunts and uncles did you have? Do you recall their names?

_____

_____

_____

_____

Were you close to your aunts and uncles? If so, what were their personalities like and what prompted your closeness?

_____

_____

_____

_____

_____

_____

_____

Do you recall special outings you had with aunts and uncles or things you did together?

_____

_____

_____

_____

_____

How many cousins did you have? Do you recall their names?

_____

_____

_____

_____

_____

Were you close to your cousins? If so, what were their personalities like and what prompted your closeness?

_____

_____

_____

_____

_____

Do you recall special outings you had with cousins or things you did together?

_____

_____

_____

_____

_____

_____

Were there other family members you were close to? Who and what prompted the closeness?

_____

_____

_____

_____

Did your extended family typically or occasionally get together for parties, holidays or reunions? What were these get-togethers typically like?

_____

_____

_____

_____

_____

_____

Can you recall a few funny, emotional, or otherwise interesting stories at get-togethers?

_____

_____

_____

_____

_____

_____

_____

_____

_____

_____

_____

_____

_____

_____

_____

_____

_____

"Families are like fudge: mostly sweet, with a few nuts."

Les Dawson

Additional Notes

Additional Notes

Section Two: Essential Elements of Childhood

Early Childhood

What pets did you have growing up? What were their names and how close were you to them?

_____

_____

_____

_____

When you were a young child, what did you want to be in terms of your career when you grew up? What about when you were in high school?

_____

_____

_____

_____

Where did you and your family typically eat dinner? Describe if it was a formal and quiet affair, if there was a lot of conversation, and what your topics did you discuss?

_____

_____

_____

_____

What were your favorite holidays when you were a child and why?

_____

_____

_____

_____

_____

How did you and your family typically celebrate the big holidays such as birthdays, Christmas, Hanukkah, or the equivalent?

_____

_____

_____

_____

_____

What are one or two of the best gifts you ever received as a child?

_____

_____

_____

_____

_____

When you played alone, what were your favorite toys, games, and activities?

_____

_____

_____

_____

What were your favorite movies, TV shows, books, songs, and musical performers when you were in elementary school? What about in high school?

_____

_____

_____

_____

_____

_____

Did you take lessons in musical instruments when you were young? How long did you stick with it, did you practice a lot, and how good at it did you become?

_____

_____

_____

_____

_____

From home-cooked meals to junk food and desserts, what were your favorite foods as a young child? As a teen?

_____

_____

_____

_____

Describe the chores you were responsible for doing in your youth.

_____

_____

_____

_____

When you were a child, what kinds of cars did your parents own?

_____

_____

_____

_____

Describe your first job outside of the home and any other jobs you had in youth (such as paper routes, mowing lawns, babysitting and the like). Do you recall how much you got paid?

_____

_____

_____

_____

What were you most afraid of in your youth, such as spiders, dark closets, or getting beat up?

_____

_____

_____

_____

_____

What was the biggest trouble you ever got into as a young child? As a teenager? What did you do and why, who found out, and what happened?

_____

_____

_____

_____

_____

_____

_____

_____

_____

_____

_____

Additional Notes

Youthful Love

Butterflies. Fireworks. Heartbreaks. Youthful boyfriends or girlfriends and those we may have wished were so, meant so much at the time, and can still spark fond smiles today.

Describe your first kiss. How old you were, who he or she was, where you kissed, and how you felt afterward.

_____

_____

_____

_____

Describe you first childhood sweetheart. How old you were, how did you know him or her, how long you were together, and any special stories the two of you shared.

_____

_____

_____

_____

_____

_____

_____

Describe the first real date you went on. How old were you, who was it, where did you go, and other interesting facts?

_____

_____

_____

_____

_____

Who were your most serious boyfriends or girlfriends through your college years? Describe them, how old you were, where you'd go together, and other memorable facts.

_____

_____

_____

_____

_____

What did your parents think of your boyfriends or girlfriends? How did they treat them and can you recall any worthwhile stories?

_____

_____

_____

_____

Describe the first time and/or worst time you recall having your heart broken by a boy or girl. Who were they and what happened?

_____

_____

_____

_____

_____

_____

_____

_____

_____

What did dating typically consist of when you were young? Where did young loves usually go on dates or to hang out together? In what ways was it the same or different from today?

_____

_____

_____

_____

_____

_____

_____

_____

_____

Additional Notes

Friends from Youth

Our friends often form some of our fondest memories from youth. We played, laughed and cried, shared secrets, and also had some of our most emotionally wrenching arguments and falling outs together.

Describe your very first best friend. How did you meet him or her, how old were you, what was he or she like, and what did you typically do together?

_____

_____

_____

_____

In all your youth (from elementary school through college), who was your very best friend? Describe them and why you'd call them the best of all your best friends.

_____

_____

_____

_____

Describe your other good or best friends growing up, such as in elementary school, high school, and college. What were each of them like and what did you do together?

_____

_____

_____

_____

_____

Where and how did you and your friends typically play when you were young? What games, toys, sports did you play and did you play inside the house, the backyard, at the park, etcetera?

_____

_____

_____

_____

Recall the worst arguments you had with best friends. What did you argue about? Was anything particularly mean or rude said or done by either of you? Did you repair the relationship?

_____

_____

_____

_____

_____

_____

Did you have any enemies, kids you couldn't get along with, or people who didn't like you as a child? Who were they and what was the problem?

_____

_____

_____

_____

_____

Did you get into any physical fights when you were young? If so, describe it. Who it was with, why you were fighting, where did it take place, and what happened.

_____

_____

_____

_____

_____

Do you know where any of your best friends from elementary school, high school, or college are today? To your knowledge, how are they doing? Did you keep in touch with them into your adult years?

_____

_____

_____

_____

Additional Notes

School Days

School is a major formative part of who we are. Not only for the formal education aspects but for the more informal lessons we learn about ourselves in relation to our peers, friends, teachers, authority figures, and society in general. This section is focused on your school days.

Where did you go to elementary school, junior high school, and high school? Were they public or private institutions?

_____

_____

_____

_____

Describe what the buildings and classrooms were like at the schools you attended. Were they small or big schools, new or old buildings? How many kids attended the school? What was the playground outside like, and what kind of desks did you sit in? Please list any other descriptions that come to mind as well.

_____

_____

_____

_____

_____

Who were your favorite teachers and what made them your favorites?

_____

_____

_____

_____

Were there any teachers you didn't like and/or who didn't like you? Why?

_____

_____

_____

_____

In terms of your grades, were you considered a good or bad student? Why?

_____

_____

_____

_____

_____

_____

_____

_____

What were your favorite subjects and classes? Which did you not like?

_____

_____

_____

_____

Elementary through high school, what did you most like to do in physical education class? What did you dislike the most? Did you have to wear a uniform?

_____

_____

_____

_____

In terms of your behavior, were you considered popular, talkative, outgoing, the comedian, the wallflower, the teacher's pet, a black sheep, or a problem child?

_____

_____

_____

_____

_____

_____

_____

What did you like the most about elementary school overall? What did you like the least?

_____

_____

_____

_____

What did you like the most about high school overall? What did you like the least?

_____

_____

_____

_____

How did you spend your summer vacations from school? What are your fondest memories?

_____

_____

_____

_____

_____

_____

_____

_____

_____

Additional Notes

Additional Notes

Homes and Neighborhoods

From apartments to mansions, farms to rough neighborhoods to well-manicured suburbs, where you grew up and the neighbors around you likely played an important role in your upbringing, viewpoints, and more.

What was the name of the town or city (and the name of the neighborhood if it had a name) where you grew up? Do you still remember your address? If you lived in more than one place, try to remember all of them.

_____

_____

_____

_____

Describe as much as you can about the home or homes you lived in as a child. Were they apartments, condominiums, single-family homes, farms? Were they older or newer, what style, and what did they look like inside and out?

_____

_____

_____

_____

_____

If you grew up on a farm, please describe it. How much land, what crops and livestock were raised there, what were the outbuildings like, and what was in the surrounding area?

_____

_____

_____

_____

Describe what the towns, neighborhoods, or areas were like. Were they big or small, wealthy or poor, safe or dangerous, busy or quiet, and any other details you can provide.

_____

_____

_____

_____

_____

What do you recall about your neighbors? Their names, young or old, and was there anything interesting or quirky about them?

_____

_____

_____

_____

_____

Did you or your family have a close relationship with your neighbors? Who were they and what types of things your families do together?

_____

_____

_____

_____

Were there neighbors with whom you or your family had rivalries or disputes? Describe what the issues were, any serious blowouts that occurred, and how things were resolved if they were.

_____

_____

_____

_____

Do you recall any particularly interesting, colorful, or outrageous characters who lived or worked in your neighborhood? Describe them and any stories you recall about them.

_____

_____

_____

_____

Were there major fires, crimes, or other disasters in your neighborhood that caused a big buzz? Describe what happened and how the neighborhood responded to it.

Additional Notes

Family Time

Describe the most memorable vacations you took with your family. Where did you go and what made the vacations enjoyable (or not enjoyable)?

_____

_____

_____

_____

_____

_____

What was a typical evening like at home with your family when you were a young child? Did this change a lot when you became an older child such as in high school?

_____

_____

_____

_____

_____

_____

Who were your heroes or idols when you were a young child? When you were a teenager?
What did you appreciate about them?

_____

_____

_____

_____

_____

_____

_____

_____

What kind of clubs and associations were you a member of in your elementary and high school
years, such as Girl Scouts, Boy Scouts, chess club, or the debate team? What were they like?

_____

_____

_____

_____

_____

_____

_____

_____

Who was the strangest or most eccentric person you recall knowing in your youth? Was it a child or adult? What was their relation to you? What made you feel that way about them?

_____

_____

_____

_____

_____

_____

Additional Notes

_____

_____

_____

_____

_____

_____

_____

_____

_____

_____

_____

_____

Additional Notes

College Years

If you attended college, where did you go? What did you major in? Did you graduate?

_____

_____

_____

Did you live in a dorm room? If so, did you like it? What do you recall about your roommates?

_____

_____

_____

Were you in any fraternities or sororities, social or academic, and if so, did you enjoy and appreciate the experience? What was the best and worst thing about it?

_____

_____

_____

_____

What were your favorite classes in college, and why did you like them?

_____

_____

_____

_____

Describe some of the wildest or craziest things you did in college.

_____

_____

_____

_____

_____

_____

_____

Did you ever win any awards or honors in elementary school, high school, or college? What were they for?

_____

_____

_____

_____

_____

_____

Additional Notes

Additional Notes

Religion

Church, religion, and spirituality have a central role in many people's lives. This often stems from what they experienced in their formative years.

What religion (if any) were you raised in? If you were not raised in a particular religion, was spirituality an aspect of your upbringing in any way?

_____

_____

_____

Were either or both of your parents very religious people?

_____

_____

_____

Do you recall the names and locations of the churches or religious centers you attended in your youth? Did you attend regularly or periodically?

_____

_____

_____

_____

Did you pray at home or participate in any religious ceremonies at home? If so, describe what you did and how often.

_____

_____

_____

_____

Describe what these churches or religious centers were like in terms of their size, what they looked like, how many people attended services, and anything else you can remember.

_____

_____

_____

_____

_____

Describe what typical religious services were like. How long did they last? Who led the services and what did you think of him or her? What type of music was played, and did you sing a lot?

_____

_____

_____

_____

_____

What was your favorite part of going to church or its equivalent? What did you dislike?

_____

_____

_____

_____

_____

If you were baptized, when and what was the ceremony? Who were your godparents?

_____

_____

_____

Describe other milestones you achieved in your religion, such as Confirmation or Bat or Bar Mitzvahs. What did you do to achieve it, what was the ceremony, and was there a gathering afterward? Add any other details you can.

_____

_____

_____

_____

_____

_____

What were your thoughts about religion, church, and God when you were young? Did you understand the concepts? Did you firmly believe or have doubts?

_____

_____

_____

_____

_____

"As long as there are tests, there will be prayer in schools."

Author Unknown

Additional Notes

_____

_____

_____

_____

_____

_____

_____

_____

_____

Sports

Sports play a central and passionate role in many young people's lives. The initial questions are geared to major sports teams or individuals you enjoyed watching, such as professional teams or boxing matches. The later questions are geared to sports you played.

Which sports did you enjoy following as a fan? What was your favorite sport of all?

_____

_____

_____

What specific teams and/or individuals were you a fan of? Did you watch games on the TV or listen to them on the radio?

_____

_____

_____

Did you ever attend live games of your favorite teams? Describe a memorable game or match you attended live. What was the name of the stadium, who went with you, and who won?

_____

_____

_____

What was one of the greatest sports games or individual feats you witnessed, whether live or on the radio or TV? Describe what happened and how it made you feel.

What sports did you participate in during your elementary and high school years?

How long did you participate? How much did you practice? How good did you get?

Did you participate in games against other teams or competitions against other individuals? What were the outcomes in terms of winning and losing?

_____

_____

_____

_____

_____

Did you win any awards or break any records in the sports you played in?

_____

_____

_____

_____

Describe the greatest games or matches you had in the sports you played. What made it such a great game for you?

_____

_____

_____

_____

_____

_____

_____

Additional Notes

Interesting Miscellaneous

Did you ever meet or know anyone you considered famous when you were young? Who was it and how did you know or meet them?

_____

_____

_____

_____

What was the very first car you ever owned? Did you buy it or was it given to you? How old were you?

_____

_____

_____

Were you ever arrested or did you ever have any run-ins with the police in your youth? Describe what happened.

_____

_____

_____

_____

What were the two or three biggest historical events that occurred when you were young? Where were you when they happened and what were your thoughts about them then?

_____

_____

_____

_____

_____

In terms of academics, sports, the arts, clubs, religious training, or otherwise, what accomplishments do you recall being proudest about in your youth?

_____

_____

_____

_____

If you could change anything about your youth, what would it be and why?

_____

_____

_____

_____

"You can only be young once. But you can always be immature."

Dave Barry

Additional Notes

Additional Notes

Section Three: Your Adult Years

Romantic Relationships

This section pertains to boyfriends or girlfriends aside from anyone you married.

Aside from anyone you married, who were your most serious boyfriends or girlfriends as an adult? How old were you when you were involved in each of these romantic relationships?

_____

_____

_____

_____

_____

Describe when and where you met each of these boyfriends and girlfriends you never married and what attracted you to them.

_____

_____

_____

_____

_____

_____

_____

What were each of these boyfriend's or girlfriend's personalities like? What did they do for a living? What was particularly interesting about them?

_____

_____

_____

_____

How and why did these relationships end?

_____

_____

_____

_____

What were the most important things you learned from these relationships?

_____

_____

_____

_____

Did you ever propose to, get proposed to, or get engaged to anyone you didn't marry? What happened to prevent the wedding from taking place?

_____

_____

_____

_____

Additional Notes

Additional Notes

Marriage Phase I

This section pertains to the person you were either only ever married to or, the person you're currently married to, or were last married to before they passed away.

What's the name of your spouse? When and where were they born?

_____

_____

_____

Describe when, how and where you first met your spouse. Describe who first approached who, what was said, and other interesting details.

_____

_____

_____

Recall your first date with your spouse. Where did you go, how did you feel about him or her on that date, did you kiss or hold hands, and any other interesting details.

_____

_____

_____

What initially attracted you to your spouse when you were still dating?

_____

_____

_____

_____

_____

_____

What do you think he or she initially found most attractive about you?

_____

_____

_____

_____

_____

Aside from your first date, what was the most memorable and enjoyable date you went on with your spouse before you were married? Describe where you went and what made it so enjoyable.

_____

_____

_____

_____

_____

When did you first meet his or her parents? When did you first really talk to them? Describe those encounters, including how you think they felt about you.

_____

_____

_____

_____

Who proposed marriage to who, how and where did the proposal take place, what was the ring like, and how was the proposal received?

_____

_____

_____

_____

Please describe your wedding or marriage ceremony.

_____

_____

_____

_____

What was the date of your wedding and do you remember why you chose the day?

_____

_____

_____

_____

Where did the wedding ceremony take place? Describe the church, park, courthouse, home, or the like. What town was it in?

_____

_____

_____

_____

Name the people in the wedding party as best as you can recall and their relation to you.

_____

_____

_____

_____

What did you wear? What did your spouse and the wedding party wear?

_____

_____

_____

_____

Describe the wedding reception. Where did it take place, how many attended, who gave speeches, was it a calm or rowdy affair, and other interesting details you can recall.

_____

_____

_____

_____

What is the funniest, most stressful, or most embarrassing story you can recall from your wedding day? Was it before or after the ceremony or reception?

_____

_____

_____

_____

_____

_____

Where did you and your spouse go on your honeymoon? How long were you there and what was particularly interesting or enjoyable (that you're willing to share, of course) from that trip?

_____

_____

_____

_____

_____

_____

_____

_____

Additional Notes

Marriage Phase II

While the previous section focused more on your wedding and the events leading up to marriage, these questions focus more on your spouse and being married.

How would you describe the character of your spouse throughout your marriage?

_____

_____

_____

_____

What if anything changed most about their character from when you were dating them and the early days of your marriage to later on in your marriage?

_____

_____

_____

What were and/or are your spouses' favorite hobbies, interests and passions?

_____

_____

_____

What jobs and careers did your spouse have during your marriage, including through today if you're still married? Do you recall the names of the places they worked? Did they do well in these jobs and did they enjoy them?

_____

_____

_____

_____

Who did the cooking in your marriage? What were the main types of meals cooked? Did you eat out a lot and where did you like to go?

_____

_____

_____

_____

Describe a typical evening together early in your marriage. Did your time together change a lot later in your marriage? If so, how?

_____

_____

_____

_____

_____

_____

_____

What type of things did you and your spouse routinely enjoy doing together, both early and later on in your marriage?

_____

_____

_____

_____

What qualities or traits did or do you most appreciate about your spouse?

_____

_____

_____

_____

What qualities or traits most upset you or grate on your nerves about your spouse?

_____

_____

_____

_____

What qualities or traits did or does your spouse most appreciate about you?

_____

_____

_____

_____

What qualities or traits most upset your spouse or grate on their nerves about you?

Describe the first home you and your spouse lived in together and subsequent homes you lived in thereafter before any children. Where were they located, what style of homes they were, the property they were located on, furnishings they had, and other details you can recall.

Did you and your spouse travel a lot together as a couple? What places throughout the state, country, and world did you two visit together?

Describe your favorite vacation with your spouse (without children) during your marriage.

_____

_____

_____

_____

Describe one of the most touching or positively surprising things your spouse did for you.

_____

_____

_____

_____

Since you've been married, has your definition of what love is and what love takes changed much from when you were a younger adult? Please explain how it has changed.

_____

_____

_____

_____

_____

"I never forget my wife's birthday.

It's usually the day after she reminds me about it."

Author Unknown

Additional Notes

Previous Marriages

If you've been married more than once, this section pertains to any and all previous spouses aside from your current or most recent one.

If you've been previously married before your current or final marriage, what were their names, when did you get married, and when did you get divorced, separated, or widowed?

_____

_____

_____

_____

Describe your previous spouses' personality, what they did for a living, and what their hobbies and passions were.

_____

_____

_____

_____

_____

_____

_____

_____

What things did you like the most about your previous spouse or spouses?

What things did you find the most challenging or disagreeable about your previous spouse or spouses?

In your previous marriages, who proposed marriage to who, how and where did the proposal take place, and how was the proposal received?

_____

_____

_____

_____

_____

_____

In your previous marriage or marriages, where did you get married and have the reception? Where did you honeymoon?

_____

_____

_____

_____

Describe a memorable vacation or outing you had with your previous spouse. Where did you go and what made it memorable?

_____

_____

_____

_____

_____

_____

Why did you get divorced?

_____

_____

_____

_____

_____

In terms of its impact on each of you, what (if anything) do you wish you'd done differently in terms of the divorce?

_____

_____

_____

_____

_____

Looking back, was the divorce the right thing to do? Why or why not?

_____

_____

_____

_____

_____

If you were widowed and have remarried, what were the circumstances of your spouse's death?

_____

_____

_____

_____

If you were widowed and have remarried, how long did it take you to start dating again and how long before you got married again? What types of feelings, such as guilt, sadness, or fear did you have to confront in order to move forward? How did you do so?

_____

_____

_____

_____

_____

_____

What are the most important lessons you learned from your previous marriages?

_____

_____

_____

_____

_____

_____

Additional Notes

Your Children

Children. They're wonderful. They're challenging. They mean the world to us and they change our lives as no one else can. In this section, you'll be answering questions about your children, including biological, adopted, step, foster children, and anyone else you've raised as your own.

What are the names, genders, and birthdays of each of your biological children, stepchildren, foster children, and adopted children?

_____

_____

_____

_____

_____

Why did you name each of your children what you named them?

_____

_____

_____

_____

_____

Where did you first learn you or your mate were pregnant and how did you receive the news? How did your mate take the news? What about with each of your subsequent children?

_____

_____

_____

_____

For any children you or your mate gave birth to, describe what you recall about the labor and subsequent birth. Where did it take place, how long was the labor, were there any complications, and any interesting or funny stories?

_____

_____

_____

_____

_____

When your children were babies, what did you find most heartwarming about them? Most unique? Most challenging?

_____

_____

_____

_____

_____

Describe the character of each of your children when they were young.

_____

_____

_____

_____

_____

What were some of your favorite things to do with your kids?

_____

_____

_____

_____

_____

Describe some of the accomplishments of each of your children when they were younger of which you were proudest.

_____

_____

_____

_____

_____

For each child, describe a situation where they really angered you.

For each child, describe the funniest thing they did when they were younger.

Throughout their schooling, what did the teachers and other school officials tend to say about each of your children? Do you recall any teacher in particular?

What did you recall about each of your children's first serious boyfriends or girlfriends? Did you like or dislike them and why?

_____

_____

_____

_____

_____

_____

What were the teenage years like for each of your children and for you in relation to them?

_____

_____

_____

_____

_____

_____

When they left home to live elsewhere for the first time, where did each of your children go (such as college, the military, or to live with friends) and what were your feelings?

_____

_____

_____

_____

_____

_____

Describe the character of each of your children today.

_____

_____

_____

_____

_____

For each of your children, what makes you proudest about them today?

_____

_____

_____

_____

_____

For each child, describe some of your fondest memories with them in recent years.

_____

_____

_____

_____

_____

_____

In what way would you say each of your children is most like you? Most different?

_____

_____

_____

_____

_____

_____

_____

Knowing what you do now, what would you change about the way you raised your children?

_____

_____

_____

_____

_____

_____

_____

_____

For each child, if there's one piece of advice you'd give them, what would it be and why?

Additional Notes

Additional Notes

Your Grandchildren

You love your grandchildren (and great-grandchildren) like your own kids, but you usually don't have to deal with the challenging parts of their lives. At least, not as much.

Where were you and how did you feel when you learned you were going to be a grandparent?

_____

_____

_____

What are the names, genders, and birthdays of each of your grandchildren?

_____

_____

_____

How would you describe the character of each of your grandchildren and great-grandchildren?

_____

_____

_____

In what ways do you think each of your grandchildren are like their mother? How are they like their father? Are they similar to you or your spouse?

_____

_____

_____

_____

_____

_____

What type of relationship have you had with your grandchildren? For example, have you been a role model, have you been distant, have you pampered them, and why?

_____

_____

_____

_____

_____

_____

Did your grandchildren spend days or overnights with you at your house? What things do you fondly recall doing together? What do you think they enjoyed about those outings?

_____

_____

_____

_____

Did you ever take any trips with your grandchildren? What was a favorite trip and what special memories about it come to mind?

_____

_____

_____

_____

_____

For each of your grandchildren, what have they done that makes you proudest?

_____

_____

_____

_____

_____

What do you hope your grandchildren remember most about you?

_____

_____

_____

_____

_____

When it comes to relationships, love and marriage, what's the best advice you'd give your grandchildren and great-grandchildren?

_____

_____

_____

_____

_____

_____

_____

_____

_____

_____

When their lives get difficult, what's the best advice you have for your grandchildren to overcome the difficult period?

_____

_____

_____

_____

_____

_____

_____

_____

_____

Additional Notes

Additional Notes

Section Four: Essential Elements of Adulthood

Enjoyment

How many of the cars that you've owned or co-owned as an adult can you recall? Which were your favorites, and which couldn't you stand?

_____

_____

_____

_____

Did your car ever break down in a dangerous area or in the middle of nowhere? What happened, and what did you do?

_____

_____

_____

_____

Aside from your own, what was the most memorable wedding you ever attended as an adult, and why?

_____

_____

_____

_____

Did you ever meet or know anyone famous as an adult? Who and how did you meet them?

What styles did you tend to dress in when you were in your twenties? Your thirties?

What are your all-time favorite TV shows, films, and movies from your twenties and thirties?

Additional Notes

Additional Notes

Family Life

In this section, you're going to recall what life was like during the primary years when you were building and raising your family.

What towns and neighborhoods did you raise your family in? Why did you choose to move there? What were these places like such as types of homes and businesses there and the types of people who lived in your neighborhood?

_____

_____

_____

_____

_____

_____

Describe the first home and the subsequent homes where you raised your children. What style of houses, older or newer, how many rooms, what was the backyard like, and what did you like most and least about living there?

_____

_____

_____

_____

Did you typically eat meals together with your family? Around the table or where? What were the topics of conversation?

_____

_____

_____

_____

_____

_____

What were weekends like when you were raising your children? What did you each do and do together? Did you regularly attend church, see movies, watch sports?

_____

_____

_____

_____

_____

_____

What types of pets did you have when raising your family? What were their names, how would you describe their character, and who in your family was closest to them and not so much?

_____

_____

_____

_____

_____

What were your favorite holidays or special days spent with your family? What did you typically do for birthdays and the big holidays?

_____

_____

_____

_____

_____

Did your family ever experience any natural disasters, tragedies, or major challenges of any sort together? Describe them, and how you handled and coped with the situation as a family.

_____

_____

_____

_____

_____

Was retaining ties to, or a sense of, you and your mate's ethnic and racial backgrounds important when raising your family? If so, in what ways did you try to do so?

_____

_____

_____

_____

_____

How would you describe your family's overall character? Were you loud and argumentative, quiet and formal, did you talk about everything, or was a lot held in? Why was it this way?

_____

_____

_____

_____

_____

_____

From liberal to conservative (in terms of political parties), what have been your political leanings in your adult years? What is it about your chosen political party that attracts you?

_____

_____

_____

_____

_____

_____

What were two or three of the biggest historical events that have occurred in your adult years? Where were you when they happened and what were your thoughts about them?

_____

_____

_____

_____

_____

Have you ever been a victim of any type of crime in your adult years? What happened, when, where, and how did you feel about it? What happened afterward? For you and to the person who committed the crime?

_____

_____

_____

_____

_____

_____

_____

Have you ever been the member of a jury in a court case? Do you recall what the case was about and the judgment? How did you feel in relation to the case?

_____

_____

_____

_____

_____

_____

_____

_____

Describe the most embarrassing things you've ever done as an adult.

_____

_____

_____

_____

_____

_____

Do you collect anything as an adult such as stamps or figurines? When did you start collecting them and what got you into doing so?

_____

_____

_____

_____

What have been some of your favorite songs and musicians in your adult years?

_____

_____

_____

_____

"Happiness is having a large, loving, caring,
close-knit family in another city."

George Burns

Additional Notes

Additional Notes

Friends in Adulthood

Good friends are the family we get to choose. In this section, you'll answer questions about the best of those good friends in your adult years.

Throughout your adult years, who would you say your best friends have been? Who are your best friends these days?

_____

_____

_____

Describe how you met each of these friends and what their character was or is like.

_____

_____

_____

What types of things did or do you enjoy doing with your friends? Do you talk a lot and if so about what? Did or do you play games or engage in activities with them? Laugh a lot?

_____

_____

_____

Did you ever have a major falling out with any good friends in your adult years? If so, what happened and what are your feelings about it today?

_____

_____

_____

_____

Describe a situation or two in your adult years where a friend helped you out in a big way.

_____

_____

_____

_____

Describe a situation or two in your adult years when you helped a friend out in a big way.

_____

_____

_____

_____

If you could thank each of your best friends for anything today, what would it be?

_____

_____

_____

_____

Additional Notes

Additional Notes

Military Members and Family

If you've been in the military, especially if you served your country in war, there's no need to tell you it can be one of the most profound periods of life. If you were the spouse, child, or close family of someone who served in the military (especially in war), the same is true.

This section is for anyone who served in the military. The second set of questions is for anyone who also served in battles or war. The final set of questions is for those whose spouse served in the military.

What branch of the military did you serve in and what were your dates of service?

_____

_____

_____

Where were you stationed for basic training? Describe as much as you can. Are there any experiences or events that particularly stand out in your memory, from the difficult to the sad to the funny? How did you feel when you first entered versus when you were finished?

_____

_____

_____

_____

_____

_____

What was the highest rank you achieved in the military? Did you earn any special honors or commendations?

_____

_____

_____

_____

What were your various titles or jobs in the military and what did you do in those jobs?

_____

_____

_____

_____

_____

What companies, divisions, or other military units were you a part of? What was your unit known for being or doing?

_____

_____

_____

_____

_____

Did you learn to use guns or other weapons? Did you learn to fly, drive, or maneuver any vehicles or special military machinery? Please describe.

_____

_____

_____

_____

Outside of war or battle, what were some of the most memorable things you experienced in the military? For example, did you jump out of airplanes, have to survive alone in the wilderness, or go through a particularly difficult training maneuver?

_____

_____

_____

_____

What cities, states, countries, and regions of the world were you stationed in during your military service? Which did you most like, which did you dislike, and why?

_____

_____

_____

_____

Describe your various living quarters. Did you live in barracks, onboard ships or submarines, or in tents? Who were your roommates and what were your living conditions?

_____

_____

_____

_____

Describe the closest friends you had in the military. Who were they, how did you get to know them, and what was their character like? Do you still talk to them today?

_____

_____

_____

_____

_____

_____

_____

_____

If you served your country in any battles or wars, please answer the following questions.

Which war did you serve in?

_____

_____

_____

_____

How long did you serve in war and what jobs and duties did you perform?

What battles were you involved in and in what ways were you involved?

What was a typical day like while you were at war? Where did you sleep, what did you eat, and what did you spend the day doing?

Were you injured while at war? What were the injuries and how did they occur? If it happened during battle, please describe the circumstances. How were you rescued and by who, where you were taken, and how did you recover from your injuries?

_____

_____

_____

_____

_____

_____

_____

_____

_____

_____

Did you witness anyone die while at war? In as much as you're willing, please describe that experience or those experiences and how you felt inside.

_____

_____

_____

_____

_____

_____

_____

What are the most difficult memories about being in the war that you're willing to share?

_____

_____

_____

_____

_____

_____

_____

Do you recall emotionally touching incidents or experiences that you witnessed?

_____

_____

_____

_____

_____

_____

_____

_____

_____

Serving your country is heroic in itself. Did you personally experience or participate in any situation considered particularly heroic or that showed exceptional bravery?

_____

_____

_____

_____

_____

_____

These questions are for those whose spouse (or close family member) served in the military. Where "spouse" is used please substitute parent, child or whatever designation they are to you.

What branch of the military did your spouse/family serve in and what dates did they serve?

_____

_____

_____

Do you recall your spouse/family's title in the military and what jobs they performed?

_____

_____

_____

_____

Did your spouse/family ever talk to you about what they did during basic training? Please describe any stories or insights he or she shared about basic training.

_____

_____

_____

_____

To your recollection, what cities, states, countries, and regions was your spouse/family stationed in during their time in the military?

_____

_____

_____

_____

Did your spouse/family ever serve in war or participate in battle? Please describe which wars and battles, where they served, and what they did. For example, were they stationed on ships, directly involved in combat, and what battles did they fight in?

_____

_____

_____

_____

_____

_____

_____

What memorable stories did your spouse/family share about being in battles and at war?

_____

_____

_____

_____

_____

_____

_____

Where did you live while your spouse/family was in the military? What kind of housing, did you live with or around other military spouses, and what was that experience like?

_____

_____

_____

_____

How often and in what ways did you communicate with your spouse/family while they were away from you in the military? How did you communicate with them while they were at war?

_____

_____

_____

_____

What were the hardest things about having a spouse/family who was in the military? Having them away at war?

Additional Notes

Jobs and Careers

It's estimated that the average person in the United States will work about 90,000 hours between the ages of 21 and 65. Work you've done throughout your life has likely had a major impact on who you are, considering how much time and energy you've invested in it. This section focuses on both the work you've done that you'd consider a job and that which you'd consider a career.

As an adult, what organizations have you worked for, what job did you do for them, and where are (or were) they located?

_____

_____

_____

_____

Did you ever launch your own businesses? If so, what type of business was it, where was it located, how long did you have it, and what happened to it?

_____

_____

_____

_____

_____

_____

In your life, what would you describe as your primary career or careers?

In this career or careers, what type of duties did you typically have to perform?

Did you become what you wanted to be when you were a child? If you went to college, did you end up with a career related to your degree?

What was the best job you ever held and why?

What was the worst job you ever held and why?

_____

_____

_____

_____

_____

Were you ever fired or laid off? Why? How did you handle the news and what did you do to get a new job?

_____

_____

_____

_____

_____

Did you ever make any big shifts from one career to another? What inspired the shift, how challenging was it, and are you glad you did it?

_____

_____

_____

_____

_____

What's the lowest amount of money you ever made in any job as an adult? What's the most money you ever made in any job as an adult?

When it comes to your work and career, what regrets come to mind? What do you wish you'd tried or done differently?

What are your proudest accomplishments in relation to your career?

Did you have to travel in any of your jobs? How often and where would you travel to? What were one or two of the most memorable business trips you took and why?

_____

_____

_____

_____

_____

_____

Did you ever have a romantic relationship with someone you worked with? Who were they, what happened, and did it present any challenges in working together?

_____

_____

_____

_____

_____

_____

If you've retired, describe your final days at work. What did you do and was there a retirement party? How did you feel about it and in the months or years beyond retirement?

_____

_____

_____

_____

What's the best advice would you give anyone choosing to pursue the specific career you chose?

_____

_____

_____

_____

_____

_____

What one piece of advice would you give to any youngster in regards to work and career in relation to their happiness?

_____

_____

_____

_____

_____

_____

_____

_____

_____

"The world is divided into people who do things,
and people who get the credit."

Dwight Morrow

Additional Notes

Additional Notes

Solitude

When you needed to step away from spouse, family, work, and all the rest for some personal solitude, where was your favorite place to go? What was your favorite thing to do?

_____

_____

_____

What were the best periods of your adult life before or during your family-raising years, and why were they?

_____

_____

_____

What were the darkest or most challenging periods of your adult life before or during your family-raising years? How did you get beyond them?

_____

_____

_____

_____

Have you had, or do you have, any superstitions that you believe in on any level (even if on a rational level you don't want to believe in them)?

_____

_____

_____

_____

_____

_____

_____

_____

How patriotic would you say you are? What do you appreciate most about your home country?

_____

_____

_____

_____

_____

_____

_____

_____

_____

Additional Notes

Additional Notes

Health and Medical

There's a lot of practical benefit for your current family and future generations by answering the health questions in this section. Share whatever you're comfortable with passing on.

What type of diseases and other health issues (including weight issues) have you encountered in your life? At what age did you first encounter each of them?

_____

_____

_____

What methods were used to treat them, such as medications, surgery, and lifestyle changes? Were the issues resolved or managed?

_____

_____

_____

If the diseases were serious or life-threatening, what emotional issues did you encounter (such as fear and anger) and how did you cope with them?

_____

_____

_____

Were you ever in any serious accidents in your life? What happened, how were your injuries treated, and what was the outcome?

_____

_____

_____

_____

Do you have allergies? If yes, which ones? What allergies run in your family?

_____

_____

_____

As an adult, what have been your worst vices (such as smoking, drinking, or eating too much junk food)? What have you done or tried to do about it?

_____

_____

_____

_____

At what age did you try your first cigarette and what were the circumstances? Have you ever been a regular smoker? If you quit, how old were you and how did you do it?

_____

_____

_____

_____

What members of your family have had cancer? Do you recall type and outcome?

_____

_____

_____

_____

_____

What members of your family have had heart disease? Do you recall type and outcome?

_____

_____

_____

_____

_____

What members of your family have had mental illness? Do you recall type and outcome?

_____

_____

_____

_____

_____

_____

What members of your family have been addicted to drugs or alcohol?

_____

_____

_____

_____

What other diseases have been diagnosed in your family?

_____

_____

_____

_____

Did you exercise regularly during your adulthood? What was your preferred method (running, yoga, weightlifting)?

_____

_____

_____

_____

Do you feel you've eaten healthy throughout your life? Why or why not?

_____

_____

_____

_____

Who is or has been the longest-living relative in your family? What do you think aided in their health and/or longevity?

What do you think the biggest secrets to a long and healthy life are?

Additional Notes

Today

These questions will give loved ones today and generations from now a look at who you are and how you live your life at the time you filled out The Truth About You.

How old are you today and how would you describe the way you feel?

_____

_____

_____

_____

_____

Describe your physical appearance right now. Include your facial features, body type, hair style, and the way you prefer to dress.

_____

_____

_____

_____

_____

What is the book you read most recently? What did you think about it?

Who do you currently live with and what's their relationship to you?

Where do you live (city, state, country)? Describe your home, neighborhood, what you like about it, and what you don't like about living there.

What items do you treasure most? These can be family heirlooms, sentimental objects, or things that are more practical. Explain why you treasure them.

Do you currently work? Where do you work and what kind of work do you do?

_____

_____

_____

What are your favorite hobbies and pastimes? What is it about them that you enjoy?

_____

_____

_____

When and where was the most recent vacation you took? What were the highlights of the trip?

_____

_____

_____

List your top three favorite restaurants and what you like about them.

_____

_____

_____

What are your favorite TV shows or recent movies?

_____

_____

_____

_____

What are your favorite reading materials, such as authors you especially love, magazines, newspapers, or websites?

_____

_____

_____

_____

If you drink beer, wine, or alcoholic drinks, what drink is your favorite right now? Has your favorite alcoholic beverage changed over the years?

_____

_____

_____

_____

Which people are you closest to today?

_____

_____

_____

_____

What is the single greatest challenge facing humanity in your opinion?

_____

_____

_____

_____

List three of your biggest fears.

_____

_____

_____

_____

What are your beliefs in terms of God, religion, or spirituality? Do you pray?

_____

_____

_____

_____

What are some of the things that give you the most peace and comfort?

_____

_____

_____

_____

What's the biggest prize you've ever won and how did you win it?

_____

_____

_____

_____

Who's the smartest person you've ever known personally and why? Who's the bravest?

_____

_____

_____

_____

_____

_____

Within your lifetime, what would you say has been your country's proudest moment and why? What do you feel is its lowest moment?

_____

_____

_____

_____

_____

_____

_____

What's been your most frightening experience with an animal in your life, whether it was someone's pet or a wild animal?

_____

_____

_____

_____

_____

What's the most expensive thing you ever bought for yourself (not because you *needed* it but simply because you *wanted* it)? How much was it and was the cost worth it?

_____

_____

_____

_____

_____

What's the most famous you've ever been? Have you ever been in the news? For what?

_____

_____

_____

_____

_____

How would you say people have most changed within your lifetime?

How would you say people have most remained the same within your lifetime?

What's the most beautiful place you've ever seen on earth? What made it so to you?

Additional Notes

Additional Notes

Section Five: Beliefs and Big Questions

This final and most important part draws on your deepest insight and wisdom culled from a life full of experiences, reflection and learning.

However conventional, controversial or emotional your responses to these questions may be, for the benefit of your loved ones (today and many generations from now), please do not hold back in sharing the truth as you see it to these questions.

Joy and Revelation

What accomplishments in your own life make you proudest?

_____

_____

_____

_____

_____

_____

_____

If you could do or try anything right now (that you never got a chance to do or try), what would it be and why did you never experience it?

_____

_____

_____

_____

_____

What have been the three to five happiest days in your life so far? Why did they make you so happy?

_____

_____

_____

_____

_____

_____

_____

What do think you've wasted the most time on that could have been better spent elsewhere?

_____

_____

_____

_____

_____

_____

_____

List the three most positively influential people in your entire life? Why?

_____

_____

_____

_____

_____

_____

_____

_____

_____

_____

What's the hardest lesson you've ever learned?

_____

_____

_____

_____

_____

_____

_____

_____

What three events in your life caused the biggest positive shifts in you? These can be something like a near-death experience, the birth of a child, a conversation with a stranger that prompted you to quit drugs, or anything at all.

If you could ask (or say) anything to any person who's passed away, who would you choose and what would you ask (or say to) them?

What three periods in your life would you say have been the darkest and most challenging? Why and what do you feel was most important in finding your way through them?

_____

_____

_____

_____

_____

_____

_____

_____

_____

What's your biggest regret in life?

_____

_____

_____

_____

_____

_____

_____

_____

What inspires your greatest feelings of gratitude?

_____

_____

_____

_____

_____

_____

_____

_____

_____

_____

_____

_____

_____

_____

_____

_____

"All I ask is the chance to prove that
money can't make me happy."

Spike Milligan

Additional Notes

Additional Notes

Character

If you could change anything about your character, what would it be and why?

_____

_____

_____

_____

_____

_____

_____

What has been the most unknown or misunderstood thing about you within your lifetime?

_____

_____

_____

_____

_____

_____

_____

What's been the biggest thing you've had to forgive and who received your forgiveness?

_____

_____

_____

_____

_____

What's been the biggest thing you've sought forgiveness for and from whom?

_____

_____

_____

_____

_____

_____

What do you miss the most about being young? What don't you miss about it at all?

_____

_____

_____

_____

_____

What have you always *preached* that you wish you'd *practiced* more yourself? In other words, what advice did you give others that you wish you actually followed in your own life?

_____

_____

_____

_____

If you could live a week being any other person currently living, who would it be and why? What if you could live a week being any person who has ever lived?

_____

_____

_____

_____

If you were given one million after-tax dollars right now, what would you do with it?

_____

_____

_____

_____

_____

Additional Notes

Beliefs

Aside from physicality, how would you say men and women fundamentally differ?

_____

_____

_____

_____

_____

_____

_____

_____

What are your beliefs about love and soul mates? Do you believe everyone has one other person they are truly meant to be with or do you believe something different?

_____

_____

_____

_____

_____

What are the most important keys to a happy marriage?

If you were to give a young adult your wisest advice about money, what would you tell them?

What have been the three most important inventions or discoveries in your lifetime and why?

Why do you think some people do bad and cruel things? Do you believe pure evil exists?

_____

_____

_____

_____

_____

_____

Do you believe in ghosts? If so, what do you think they are? Describe any first-hand experiences you've had with what you believe were ghosts.

_____

_____

_____

_____

_____

_____

Do you believe there's (intelligent) life on other planets? Why or why not? Describe any first-hand experiences you've had with UFOs, aliens, or extraterrestrial events.

_____

_____

_____

_____

_____

Why do you believe we dream? Have you had any recurring dreams throughout your life? What do you think it means?

Do you believe in God? Why or why not?

Why do you believe we exist in the first place? Why are we here?

Where do you believe we go after we die? What do you believe takes place there?

_____

_____

_____

_____

_____

_____

What would you say are the most important keys to living a happy life?

_____

_____

_____

_____

_____

_____

_____

_____

_____

_____

_____

_____

_____

Additional Notes

Hope and Vision

What are the most important things you intend to do with the rest of your life?

_____

_____

_____

_____

_____

_____

What are your greatest hopes for your country and the human race?

_____

_____

_____

_____

_____

_____

_____

_____

What are your greatest hopes for your children?

_____

_____

_____

_____

_____

_____

_____

_____

_____

What are your greatest hopes for your grandchildren and great-grandchildren?

_____

_____

_____

_____

_____

_____

_____

If you could choose a final memory before you pass away, a memory from absolutely any point in your life, what memory would you choose?

When you pass away, where do you hope you go, who do you hope to see there, and what do you hope to do there?

Assuming your blood relations will read (or listen to) this journal hundreds of years from now, what are your greatest hopes for them and the world they're living in?

When you pass away, what aspects of your character and life would you most like family and friends to remember?

Additional Notes

A Final Word

You've reached the end of the guided journal for your life story. No matter how many questions you answered, you should feel wonderful about creating this priceless gift for family now and for future generations.

Of course as long as you're here, your story is not done. So whether you think of other things from your past you want to add, or you want to include the new stories to come in your life, please do so! You can use the additional note pages in this book toward that end or continue making new audio or video recordings.

I hope that the memories you traveled were peaceful ones, and if they were not, I hope you found closure by looking at them with fresh eyes. *Your life story…the ultimate gift.*

This life story was completed by _____ **(print**

your full name) on _____ **(print full date).**

Write a personal note below if you plan to give this journal as a gift.

_____

_____

_____

_____

"You can complain because roses have thorns,
or you can rejoice because thorns have roses."

Ziggy

Additional Pages for Your Notes

Additional Notes

Additional Notes

Additional Notes

Additional Notes

Additional Notes

Additional Notes

Additional Notes

Additional Notes

Additional Notes

Additional Notes

Additional Notes

Additional Notes

Additional Notes

Additional Notes

Additional Notes

Additional Notes

Additional Notes

Additional Notes

Additional Notes

Brian Vaszily

Additional Notes

About Brian Vaszily

Brian Vaszily is the author of several other books, including the #1 bestseller, "**The 9 Intense Experiences: An Action Plan to Change Your Life Forever**" (Wiley, 2011).

A recognized expert in the areas of personal and professional growth, he's done extensive public speaking, been featured on ABC, NBC, CBS and other major media, and has built multiple successful businesses.

He serves as a director with **The Truth About Cancer**. Brian has also been an executive and life coach, performed stand-up comedy, improvisation, and acting, even appearing in his own brief scene in the film *Transformers: Dark of the Moon*.

He adores his family, including his wife and four children, and can typically be found in his garden if you can't find him elsewhere.